I0485434

First Printing, 2015

ISBN 978-1518733529

This page has been intentially left blank.

Alphabet Art: Find and Color:

This book contains hand made drawings of each letter of the alphabet.

Each letter is filled to bursting with smaller drawing all of which start with the particular letter.

A list of items to find has been provided with each letter. See how many you can find ?

Some are easier to find than others, so the list is split into those that I think you should be able to find without too much problem and those that I think only the eagled eyed may spot. Of course you may not agree with my list.

For some of them (especially the some letters such as Q, X and Z) you may need to break out the dictionary. I know I had to !

However, remember that coloring is all just for a bit of fun … So just find as many as you can and enjoy coloring this book.

A is for:

Easy to Spot			
Ace	Angel	Astronaut	
Aardvark	Ant	Athlete	
Acorn	Ant eater	ATM	
Airplane	Ape	Australia	
Albatross	Apple	Autograph	
Album	Ark	Automoblie	
Alligator	Armadillo	Avocado	
Anchor	Arrow	Axe	

Eagle Eyed			
Abacus	Alps	Aristocrat	
Acrobat	Animals	Arm	
Agate	Ankle	Asparagus	
Alien	Apron	Atlas	
Alpaca			

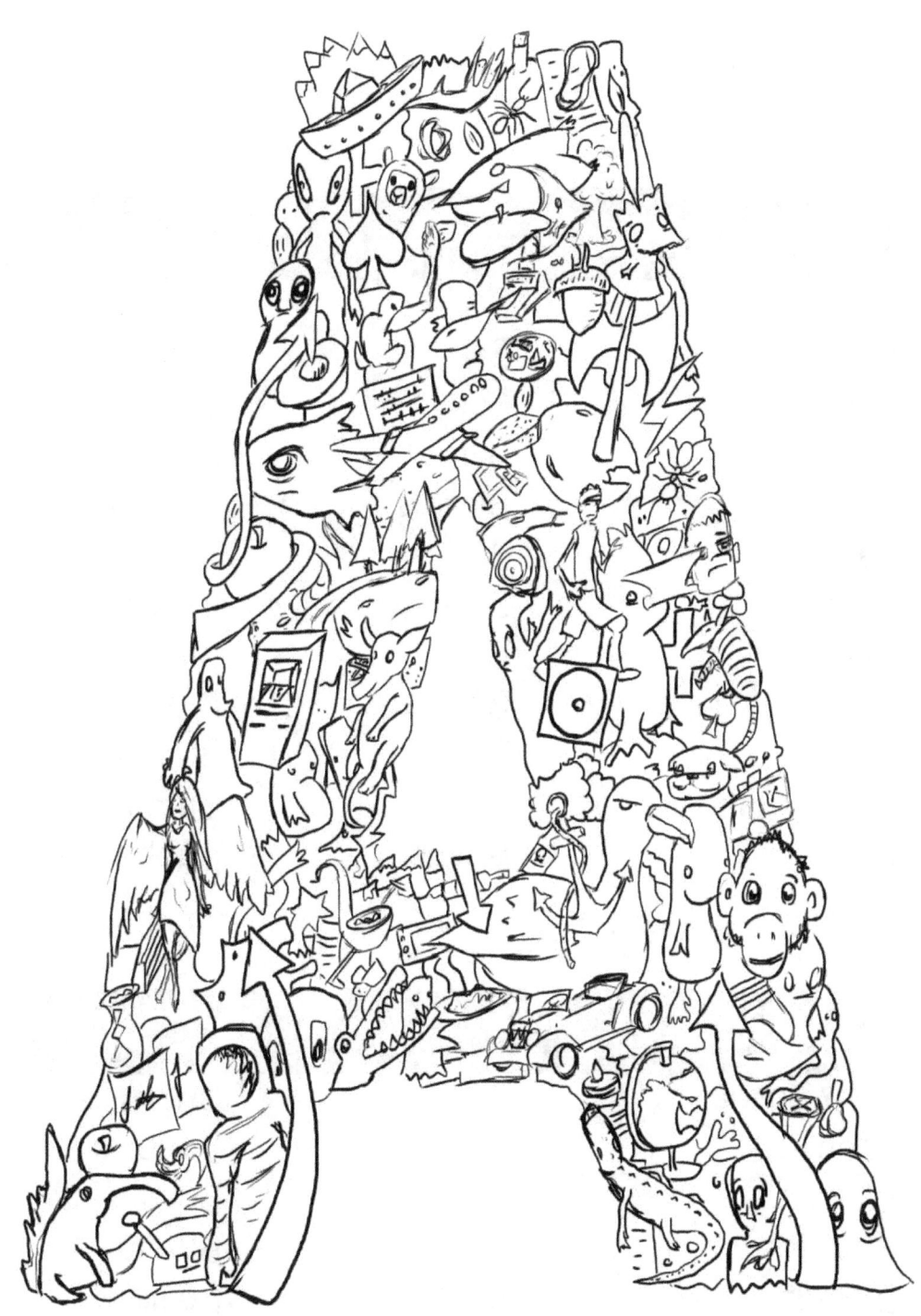

B is for:

Easy to Spot

Baboon		Bed		Bow	
Baby		Bee		Bowl	
Ball		Bell		Box	
Ballerina		Belt		Bread	
Balloon		Berries		Britain (flag)	
Banana		Bib		Broccoli	
Banjo		Bingo		Broom	
Barbecue		Bird		Bucket	
Baseball		Blanket		Bus	
Basket		Boat		Butterfly	
Basket Ball		Book		Button	
Bat		Bottle		Bubble Wrap	
Bear					

Eagle Eyed

Baby Bottle		Bone		Breakfast	
Bean		Bonnet		Bubbles	
Bicycle		Boot		Bug	
Biscuits		Boy		Burrito	
Blocks		Bracelet		Bugle	
Blueberries					

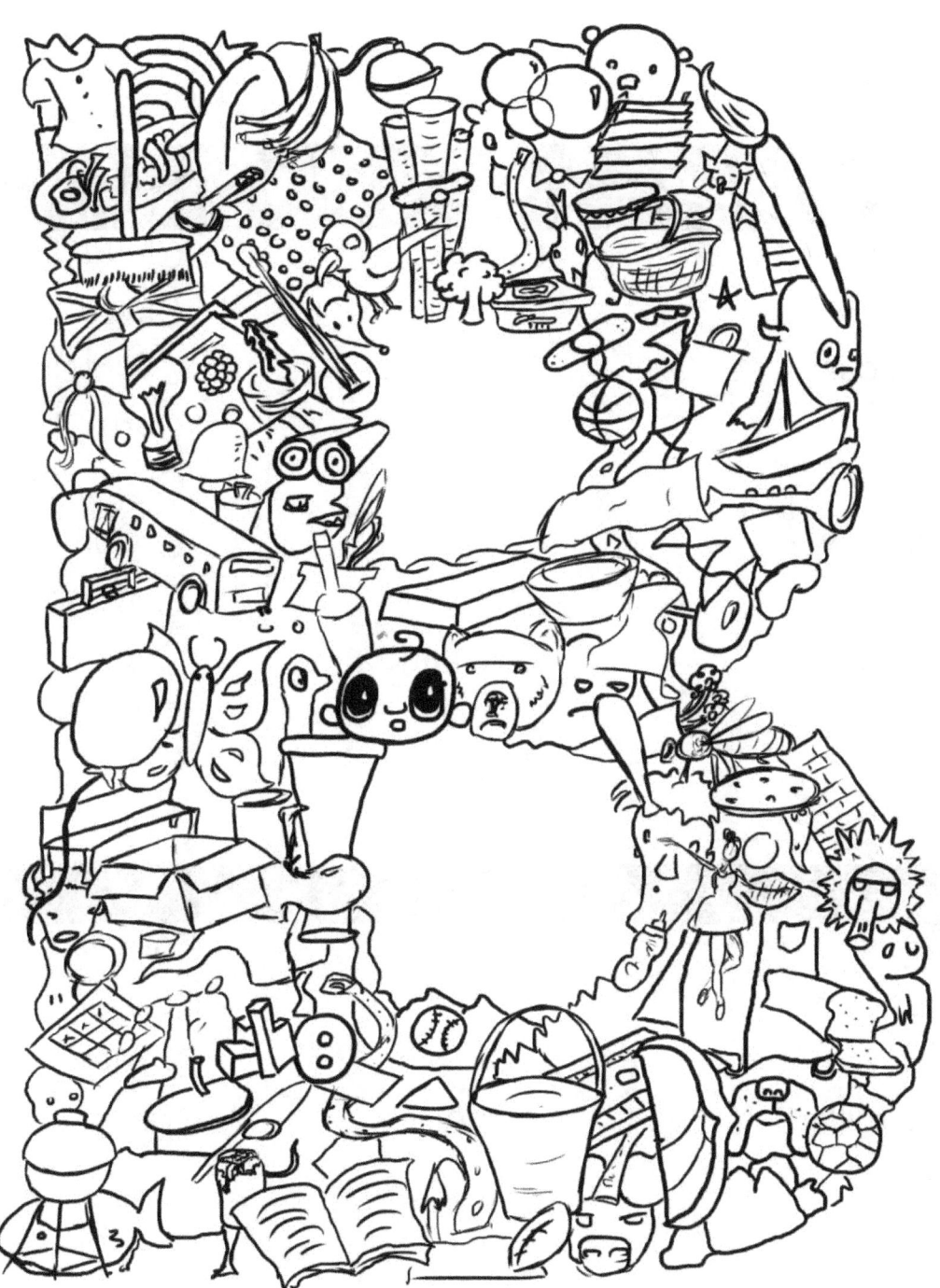

C is for:

Cactus	Carpet	Cloud
Cake	Carpet Python	Clown
Calendar	Carrot	Cocktail
Camel	Cat	Corn Chips
Camera	Cherry	Crab
Campfire	Chess	Crown
Can	Chick	Cucumber
Candle	Chimpanzee	Cup
Canon	Clock	Cupcake
Car	Clothes	

Cape	Cheese	Corn
Capsicum	Chicken	Cow
Card	Coat	Cracker
Caterpillar	Cookie	Crate
Celery		

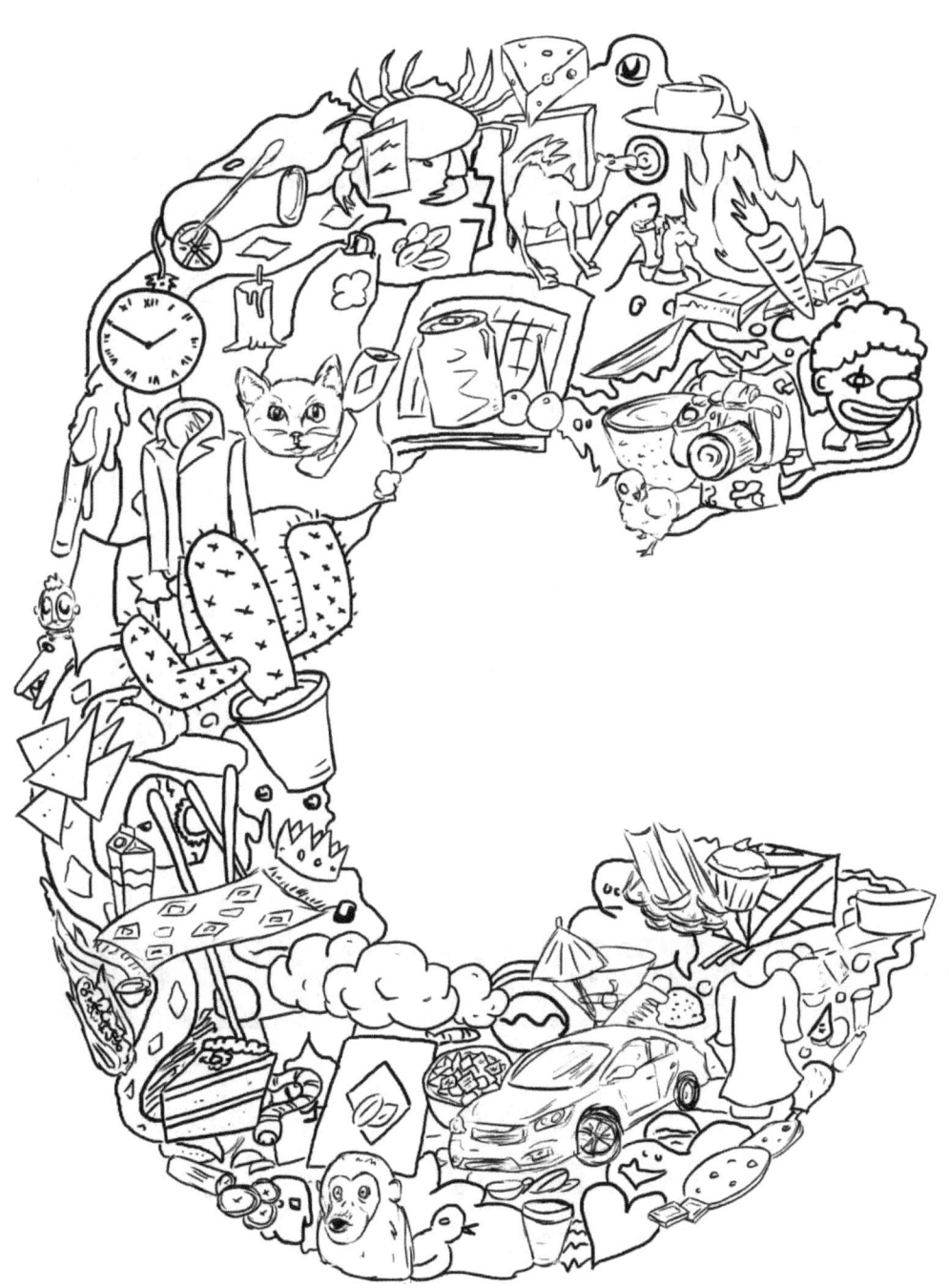

D is for:

Easy to Spot			
Daffodil	Diamonds (suit)	Dollar	
Dagger	Diaper	Dolphin	
Daisy	Dice	Dominoes	
Dartboard	Didgeridoo	Dragonfly	
Death	Dime	Dummy	
Deer	Dinosaur	Dunes	
Degree	Dish	Donkey	
Desk	Doctor	Donut	
Dessert	Dodo	Door	
Diamond	Dog		

Eagle Eyed			
Dandelion	Dove	Druid	
Dates	Dragon	Drum	
Dill	Drawing	Dryer	
Dip	Dream	Duck	
Dirt	Dress	Dynamite	
Doll	Drone		

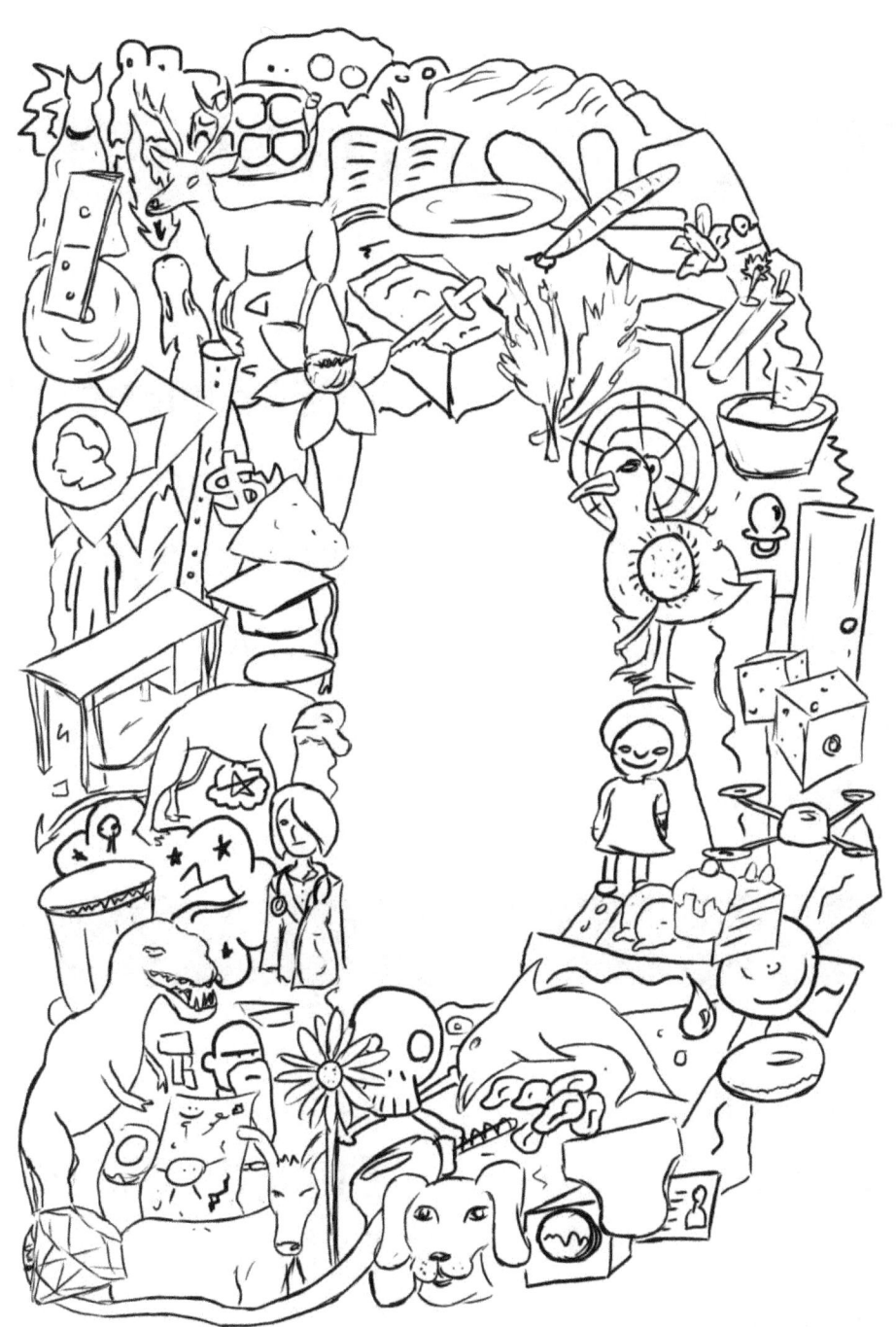

E is for:

Easy to Spot			
Eagle		Elephant	
Ear		Emu	
Earmuffs		Engagement Ring	
Earth		Envelope	
Easel		Equals Sign	
Echidna		Eskimo	
Egg		Eye	
Egg Beater			

Eagle Eyed			
Earphones		Elf	
Ectoplasm		Email	
Eggplant		England (flag)	
Elbow		Exhaust	
Electron		Eyepatch	

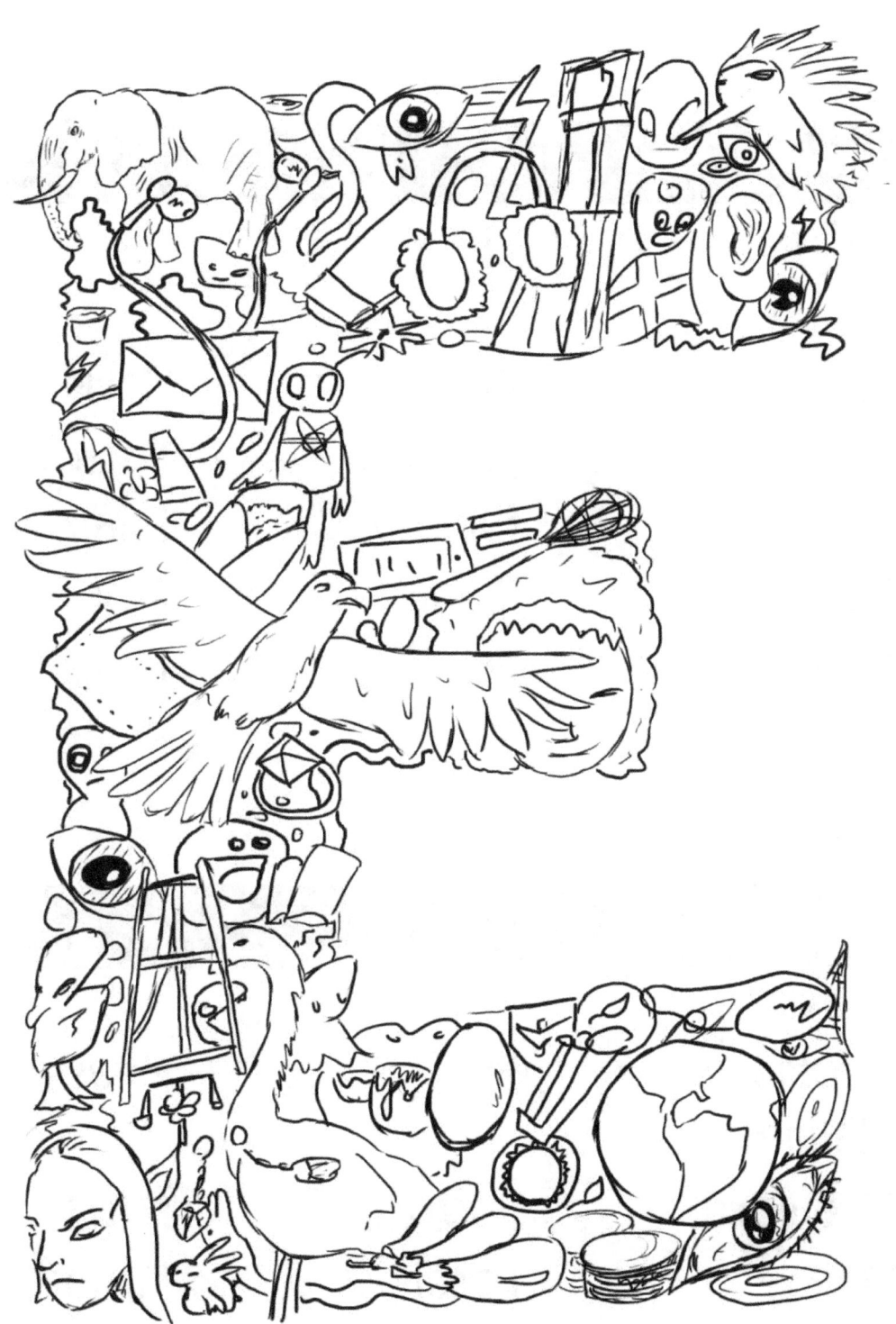

F is for:

Easy to Spot			
Face	Firetruck	Foot	
Fairy	Fish	Fork	
Fan	Five of Diamonds	Four of Diamonds	
Farm	Flame	Fox	
Fern	Flamingo	Frog	
Fire	Flower	Fruit	

Eagle Eyed			
Feather	Flute	Frankfurter	
Fireman's Helmet	Fly	Fries	
Firework	Football	Fudge	
Flag	Fossil	Funnel	

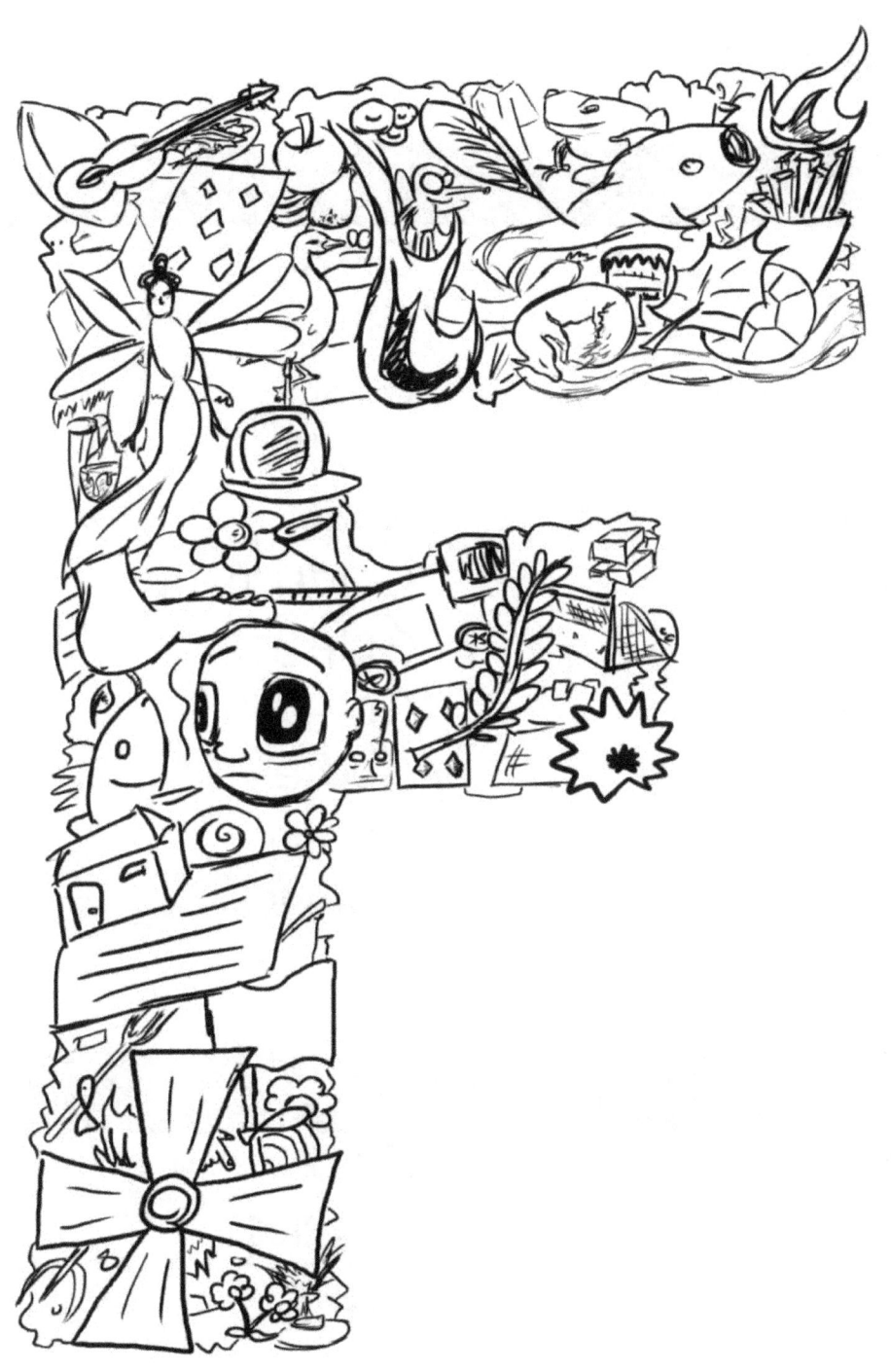

G is for:

Easy to Spot		
Game	Glove	
Garlic	Glue	
Gate	Goal	
Gen	Goblet	
Ghost	Goat	
Gift	Goldfish	
Gin	Golf Ball	
Giraffe	Golf Club	
Girl	Goose	
Glass	Gorilla	
Globe	Grapes	

Eagle Eyed		
Garbage	Gold	
Garden	Goggles	
Glitter	Grass	

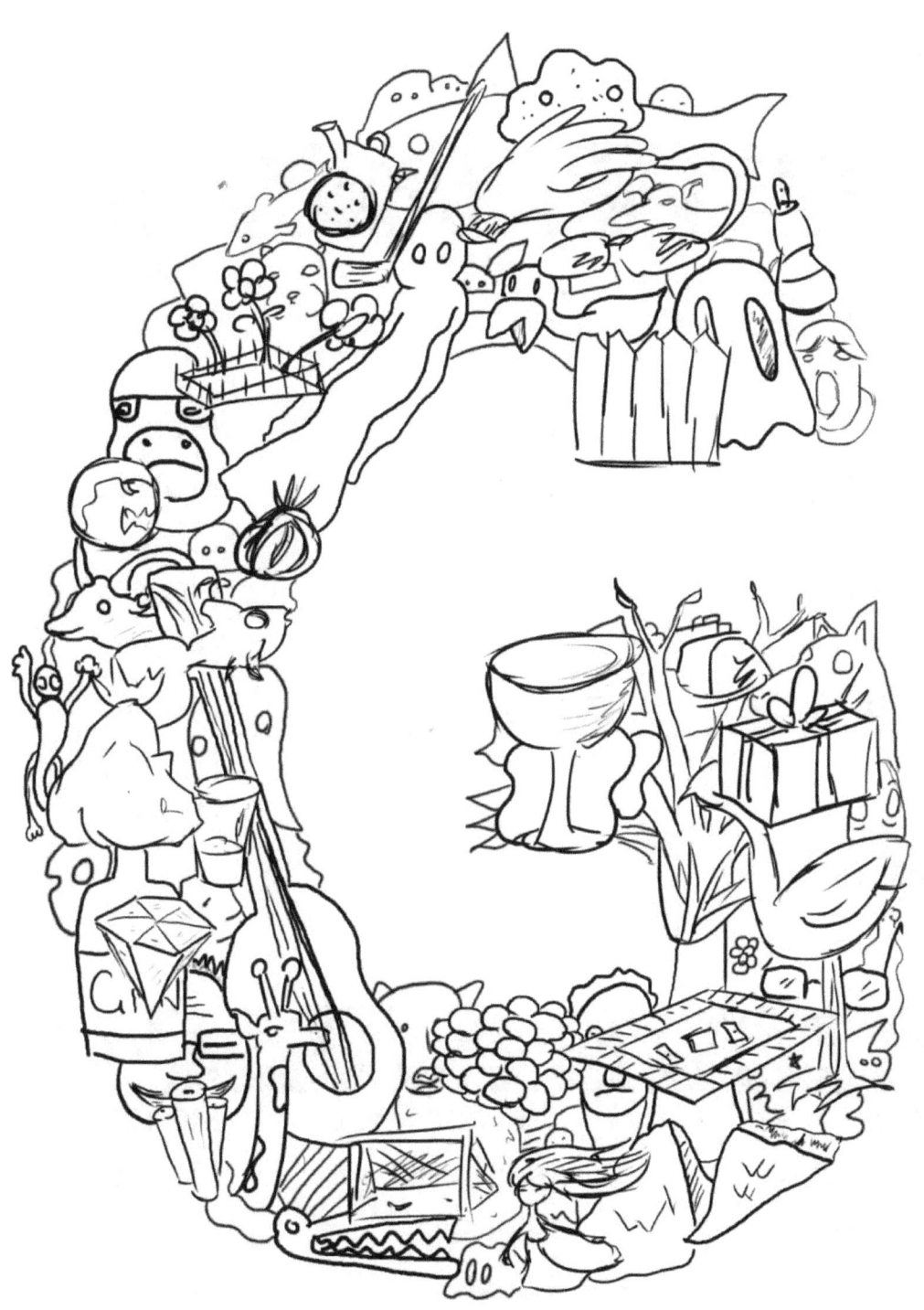

H is for:

Hammer	Head	Holly	
Hammerhead Shark	Heart	Horn	
Hand	Hedgehog	Horse	
Handbag	Helicopter	Horseshoe Crab	
Happy	Her	Horseshoe	
Hare	Heron	House	
Harp	High Heels	Human	
Hat	Hippo	Humpback Whale	
Hatchet			

Hamburger	Hermit Crab	Honey	
Hammock	Hexagon	Hotdog	
Hamster	High-rise	Hourglass	
Hand Puppet	Hills	Hummingbird	
Headstone	Himalayas		

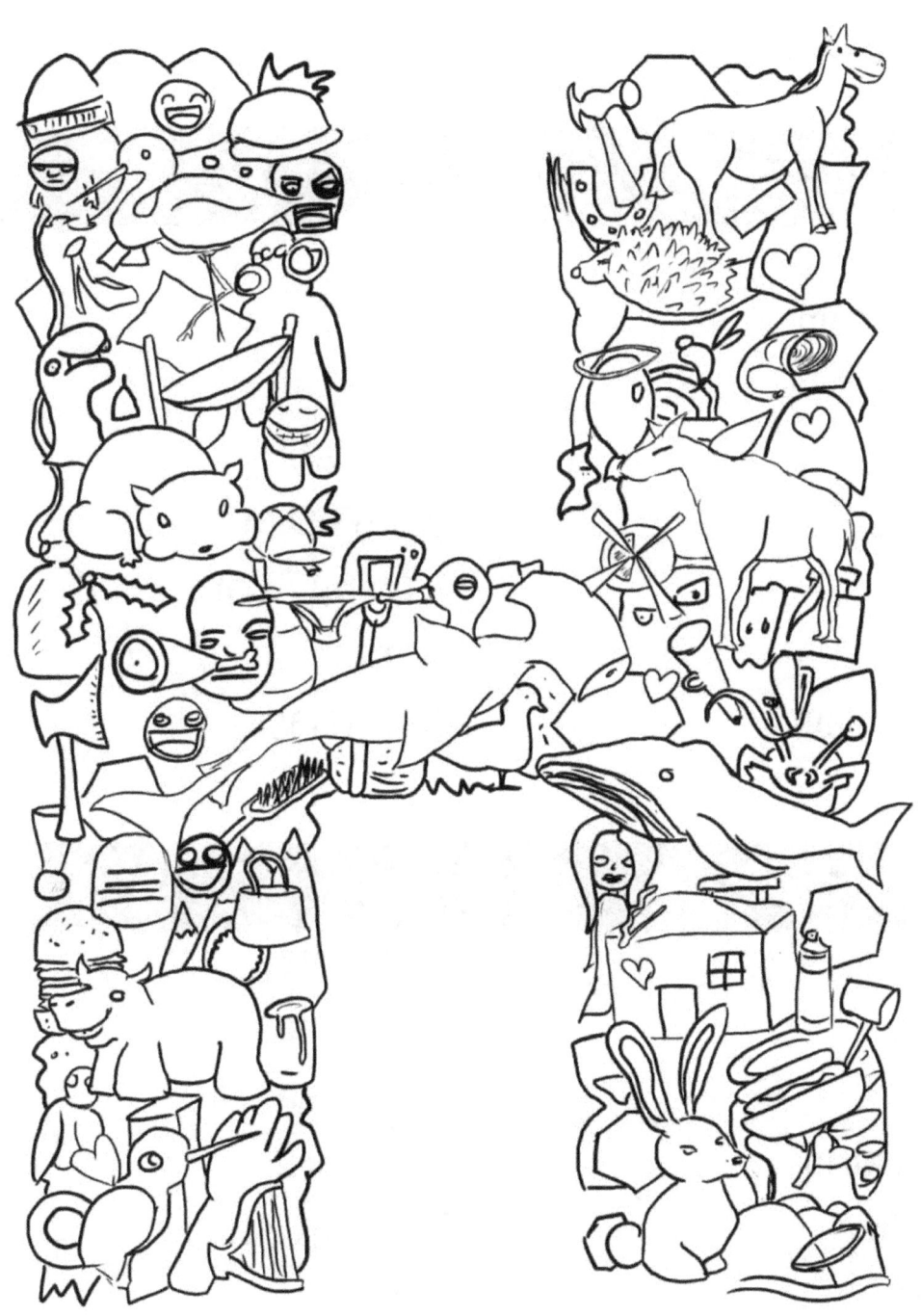

I is for:

Easy to Spot

Ibis	Ink	
Ice Cream	IPad	
Idea	IPod	
Igloo	Iris (eye)	
Iguana	Iris (flower)	
Ill	Ironing Board	
Inch	Island	
India (flag)	Italy (flag)	

Eagle Eyed

Ice Cube	Insomnia	
Icicle	Instrument	
Ignite	Intersection	
Inchworm	Invoice	
Infant	IPhone	
Injection	Iron	

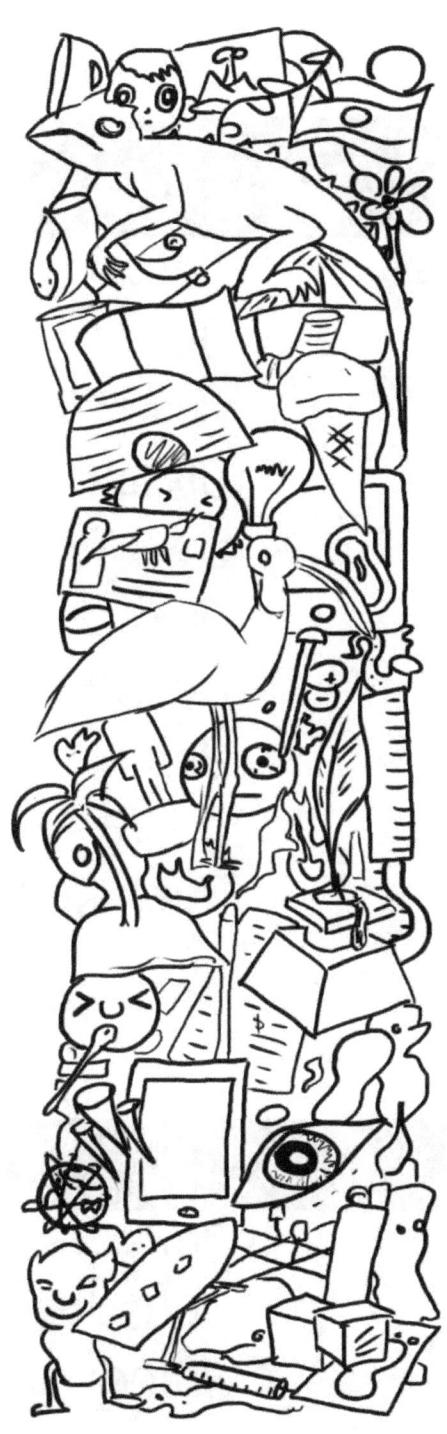

J is for:

Easy to Spot		
Jacaranda (Tree)	Jester	
Jack Russell	Jet	
Jackal	Jewel	
Jacket	Jigsaw	
Jack-in-the-box	Jolly Roger (flag)	
Jaguar	Joy	
Japan (flag)	Judge	
Jar	Jug	
Jelly	Juice	
Jellybean	Junk Ship	
Jellyfish		

Eagle Eyed		
Jail	Joker	
Jaw	Jousting stick	
Jewellery	Juice	
Joint		

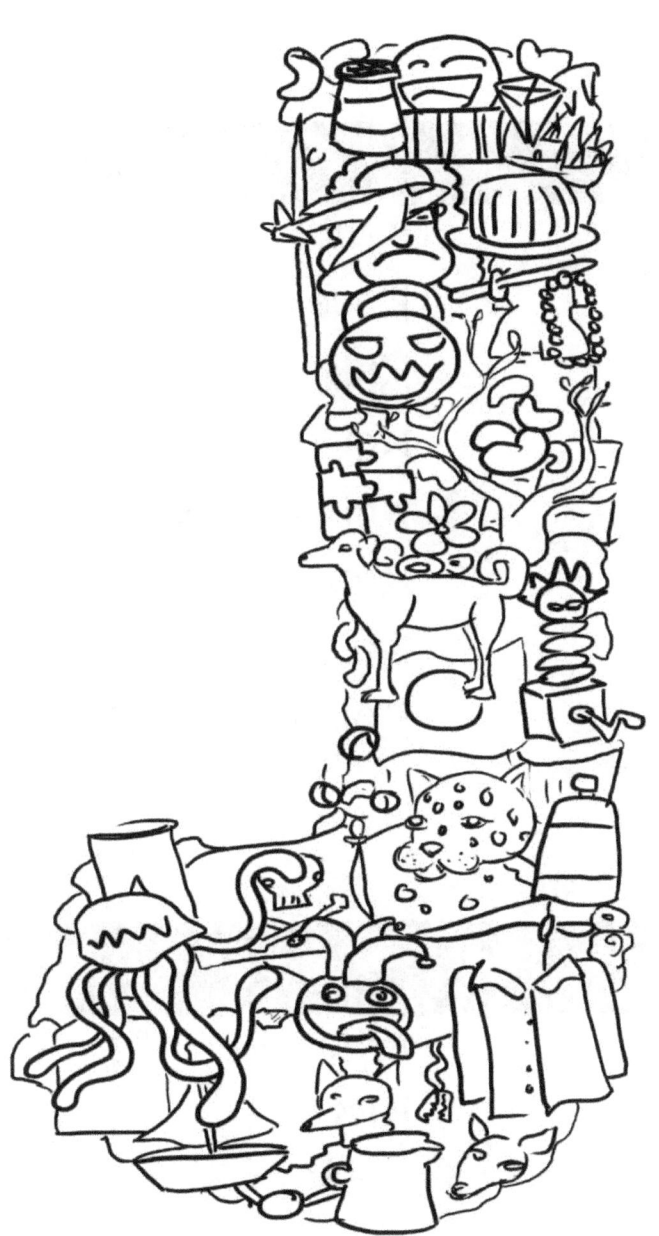

K is for:

Easy to Spot		
Kangaroo	Kiwi	
Kayak	Knee	
Kennel	Knife	
Kettle	Knight	
Keyboard	Knight (chess)	
Kid	Knot	
King	Koala	
Kite	Komodo Dragon	
Kitten		

Eagle Eyed		
Kaleidoscope	Kindle	
Kart	Kiss	
Keg	Kit Kat	
Ketchup	Kiwifruit	
Kilt	Knitting	
Kimono	Krill	

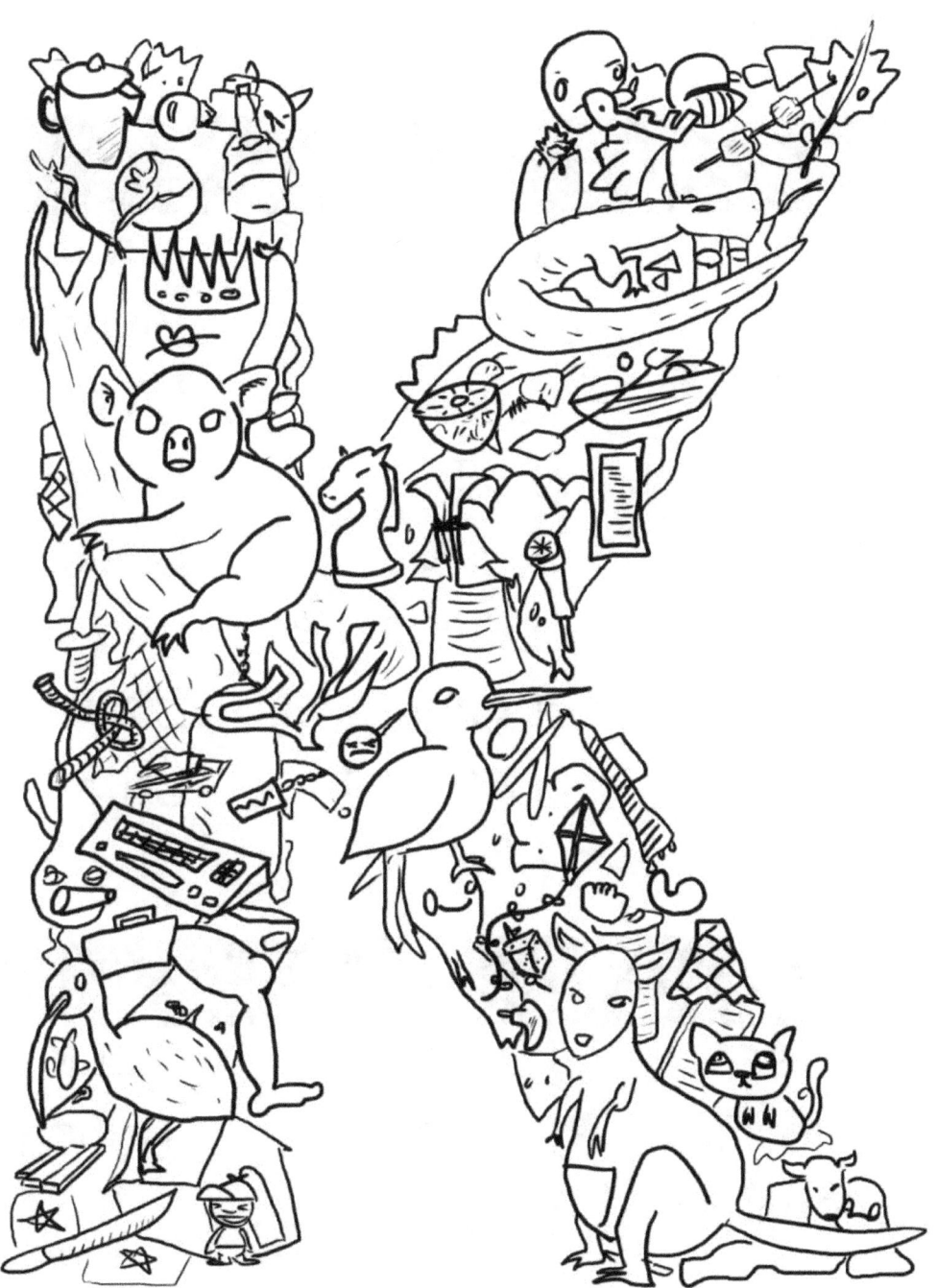

L is for:

Easy to Spot

Label		Lasso		Level	
Labrador		Lava		Lightbulb	
Ladder		Leaf		Lion	
Ladle		Leg		Lionfish	
Ladybug		Lemon		Llama	
Lamp		Lemonade		Louse	
Lantern		Lemur		Love	
Laptop		Leopard		Lynx	

Eagle Eyed

Latitude		Letter		Lock	
Lawnmower		Lightning		Lunch	
Leprechaun		Lizard			

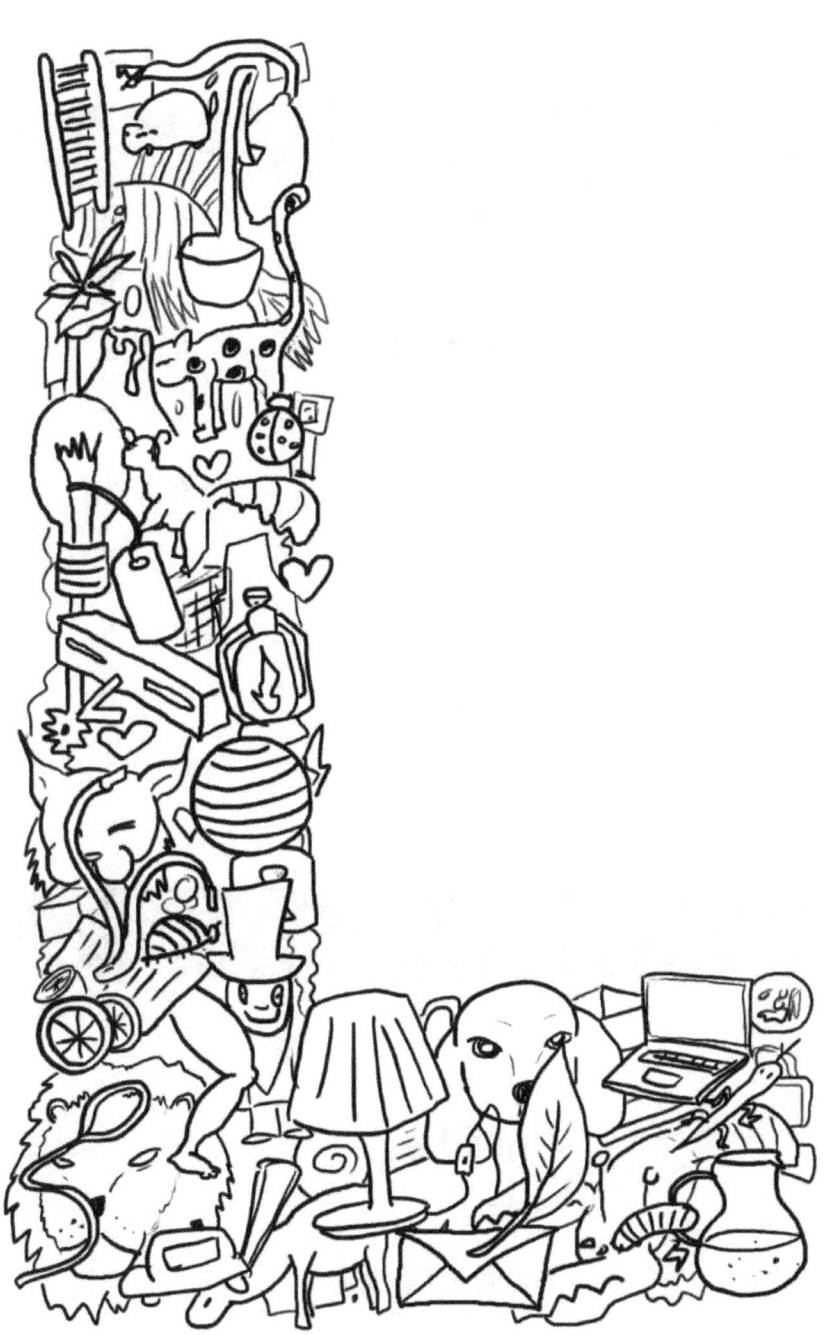

M is for:

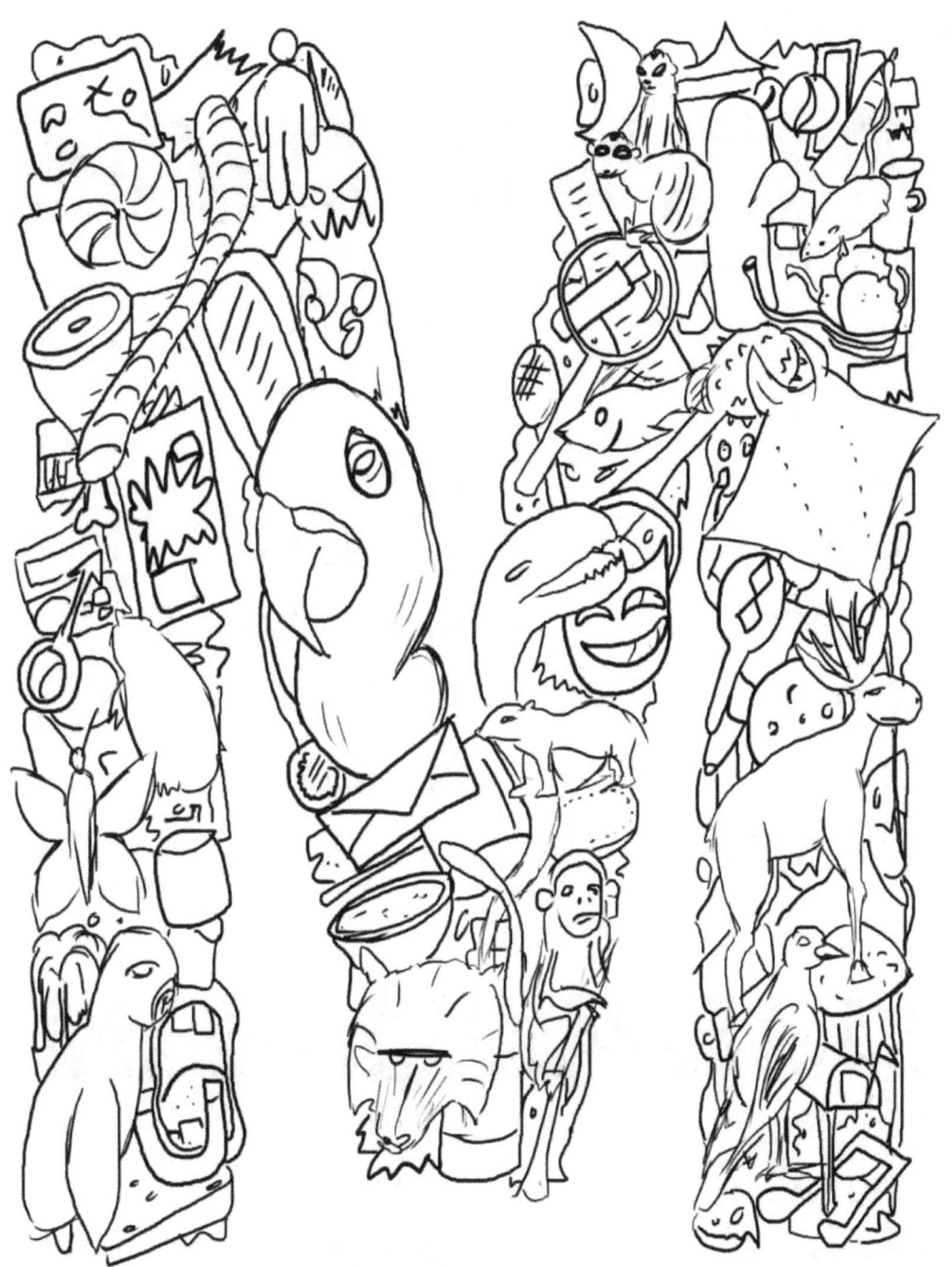

N is for:

Easy to Spot		
Nail (finger)	Newt	
Nail (metal)	Night	
Nametag	Noodles	
Napkin	Nose	
Nappy	Notepad	
Necklace	Noticeboard	
Necktie	Novel	
Net	Numbat	
Newspaper		

Eagle Eyed		
Nachos	Ninja	
Narwhal	Note	
Nectarine	Nuclear	
Neptune	Nut	

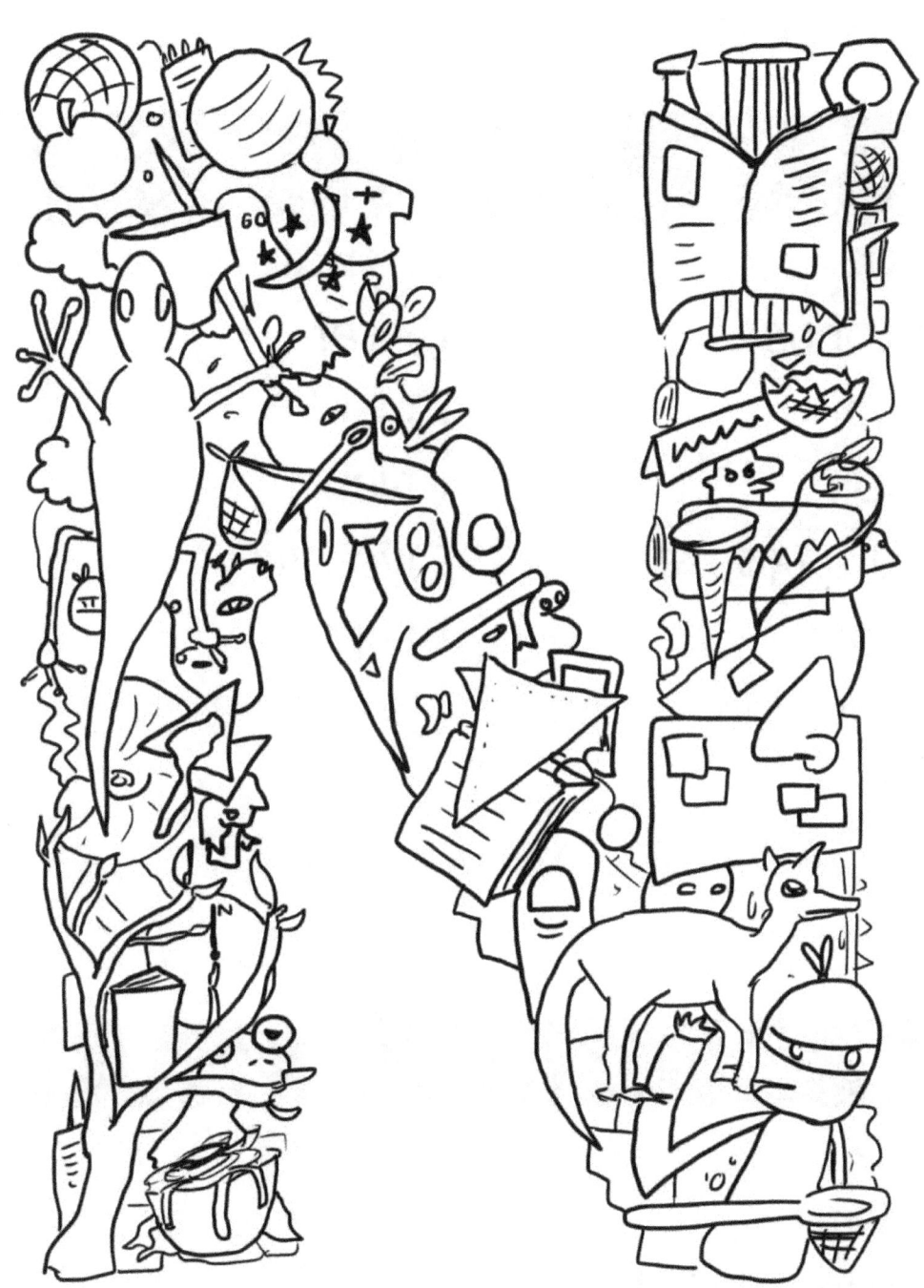

O is for:

Easy to Spot		
Oboe	Ostrich	
Octopus	Otter	
Okapi	Oval	
Onion	Oven	
Opera House	Overalls	
Orange	Owl	
Orangutan	Ox	
Orbit	Oyster	
Orca		

Eagle Eyed		
Oats	Octave	
Ocean	Old	
Ocean Sunfish	Olive	
Octagon	Opera	

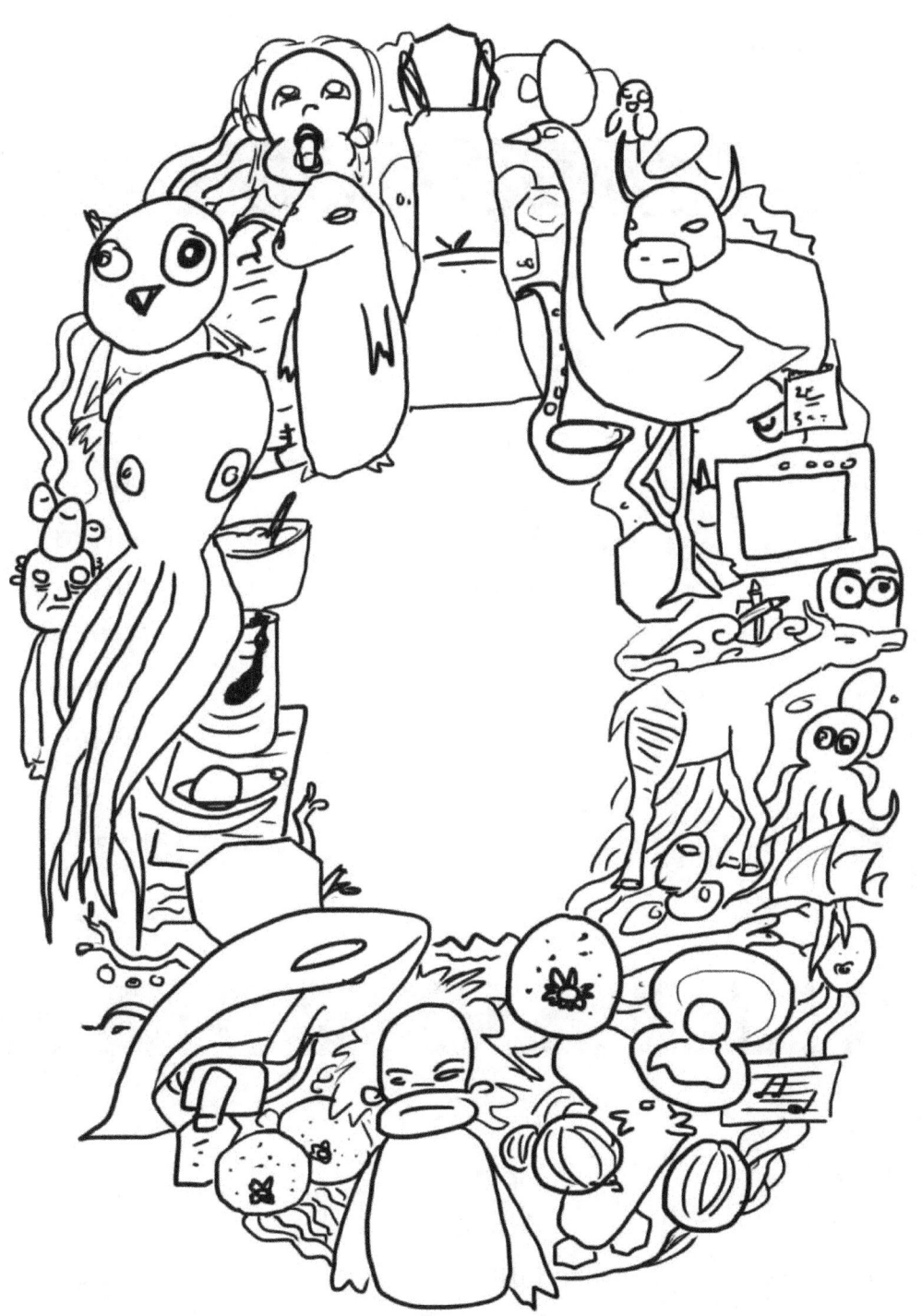

P is for:

Easy to Spot

Package		Pear		Poodle	
Paddle		Pelican		Popcorn	
Padlock		Penguin		Porcupine	
Palm Tree		Penny		Postcard	
Panda		Pepper (capsicum)		Present	
Panther		Pig		Princess	
Pants		Pineapple		Pufferfish	
Parachute		Pirate		Puffin	
Parrot		Pizza		Pug	
Party hat		Platypus		Pumpkin	
Pawn		Poison Dart Frog		Puppy	
Peach		Polar Bear		Puzzle	
Peacock		Pond Skater		Pyramid	
Peanut					

Eagle Eyed

Pan		Picture		Possum	
Parallelogram		Pine Cone		Pot	
Pencil Case		Plant		Prawn	
Pentagon		Plasma		Pretzel	
Pepper (spice)		Plum		Puppet	
Piccolo		Pocket		Pyjamas	
Pickles		Poltergeist			

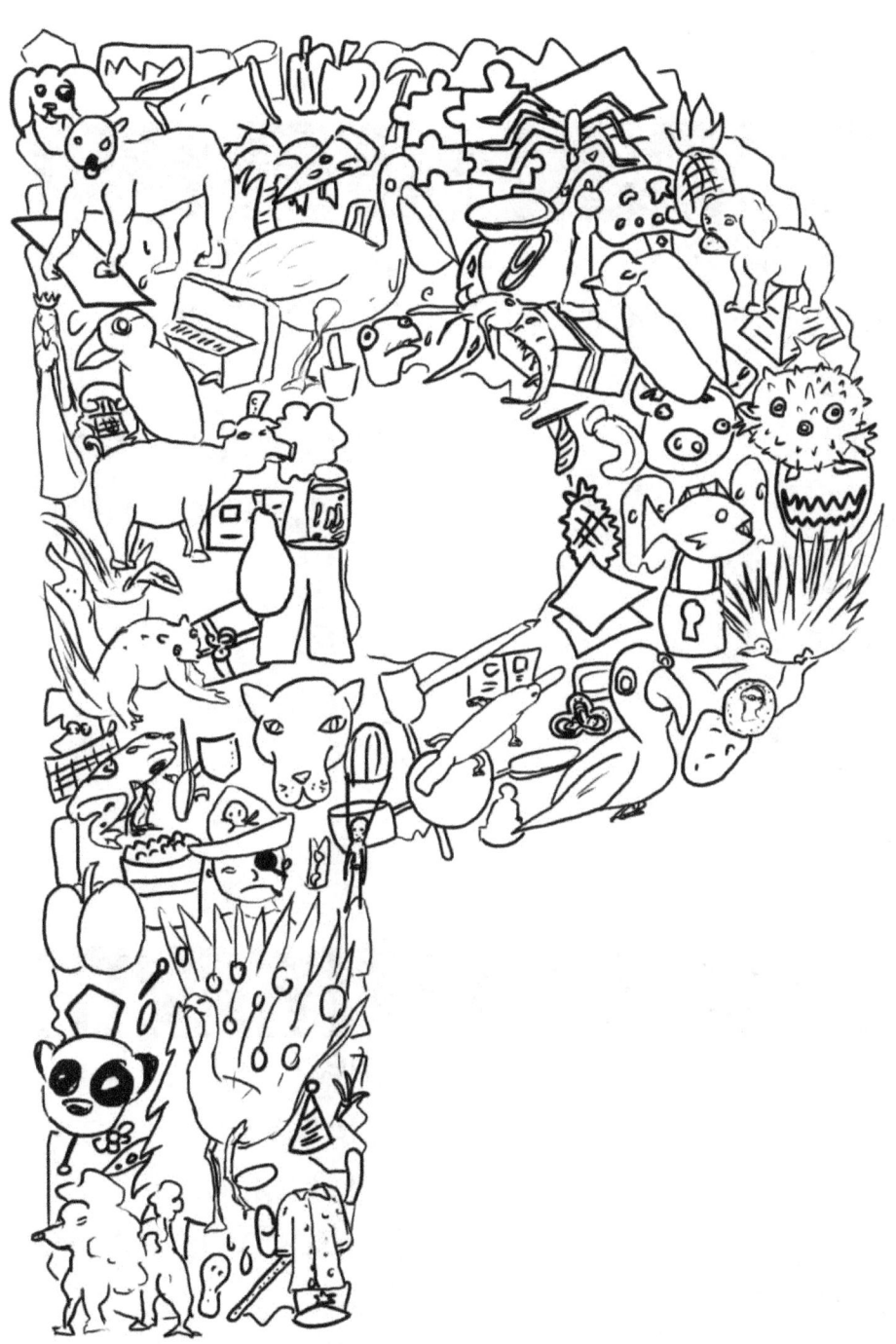

Q is for:

Easy to Spot			
Quadruplets		Queen (chess piece)	
Quagga (extinct horse)		Queen Bee	
Quail		Queztalcoatlas (prehistoric reptile)	
Quail Egg		Quill	
Quarter		Quiz	
Quartz		Quokka	
Quaver		Quoll	
Queen			

Eagle Eyed			
Quadrant		Quest	
Quadratic		Quetzal	
Quadriceps		Quetzalcoatl (Mesopotamian God)	
Quadruped		Quilt	
Quebec (flag)		Quinoa	
Queensland		Quote	

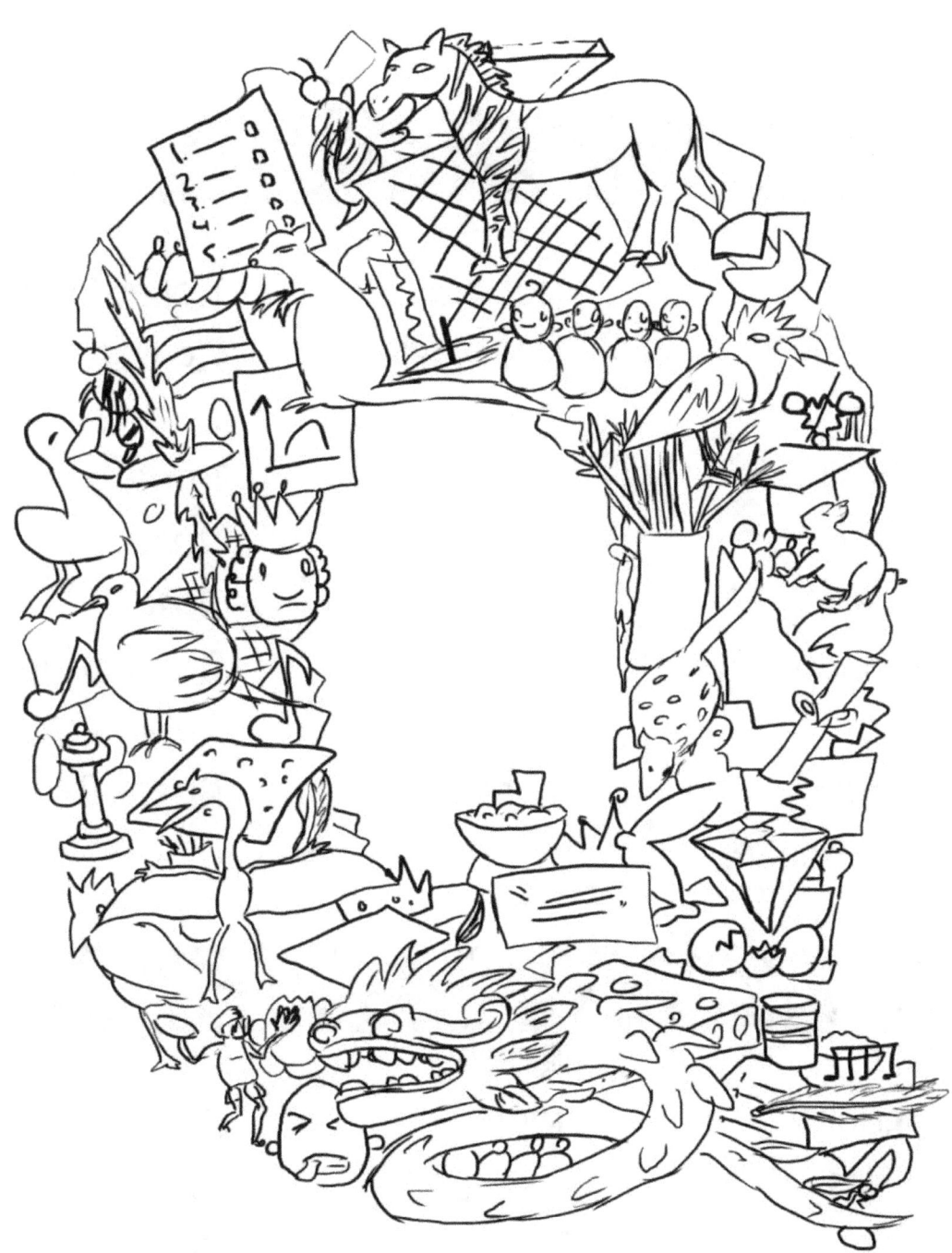

R is for:

Easy to Spot							
Rabbit		Receipt		Rocket			
Racket		Record		Roller Skates			
Racoon		Rectangle		Rolling Pin			
Radio		Refrigerator		Rooster			
Rain		Reindeer		Rope			
Raincoat		Revolver		Rosary			
Rake		Rhino		Rose			
Raspberry		Ribbon		Rubber Duck			
Rat		Robin		Rubik's Cube			
Rattle		Robot		Rugby Ball			
Rattlesnake							

Eagle Eyed							
Raft		Relish		Rock			
Ragdoll		Rice		Roll			
Raisins		Rice Ball		Rug			
Ravioli		Ring		Ruler			
Razor							

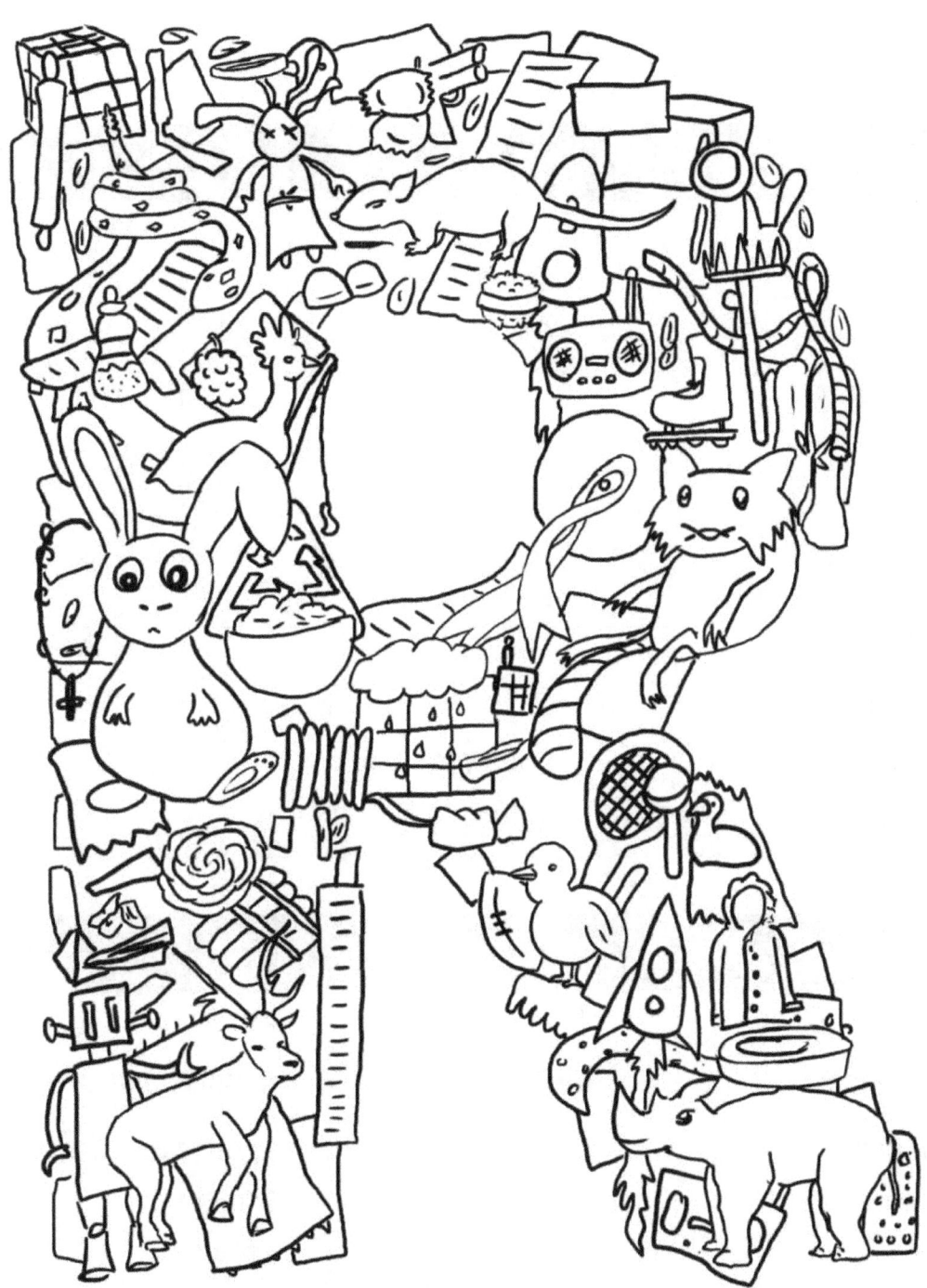

S is for:

Easy to Spot

Sabre-toothed Cat		Seal		Spoon	
Sailboat		Serval (Cat)		Square	
Salt		Shark		Squid	
Sandwich		Sheep		Squirrel	
Saw		Shirt		Stamp	
Scarf		Shoe		Star	
Scorpion		Siamese Fighting Fish		Starfish	
Sea Dragon		Snail		Stick Insect	
Sea Lion		Snake		Sun	
Sea Urchin		Soup (Bowl of)		Suit	
Seahorse		Spider			

Eagle Eyed

Salad		Seed		Spikes	
Salamander		Shrimp		Sponge (animal)	
Sandcastle		Siamese Cat		Sponge (household)	
Scissors		Sloth		Stingray	
Sea		Soap		Stoat	
Sea Slug		Sock		Suitcase	
Seaweed		Sparrow		Sunbear	

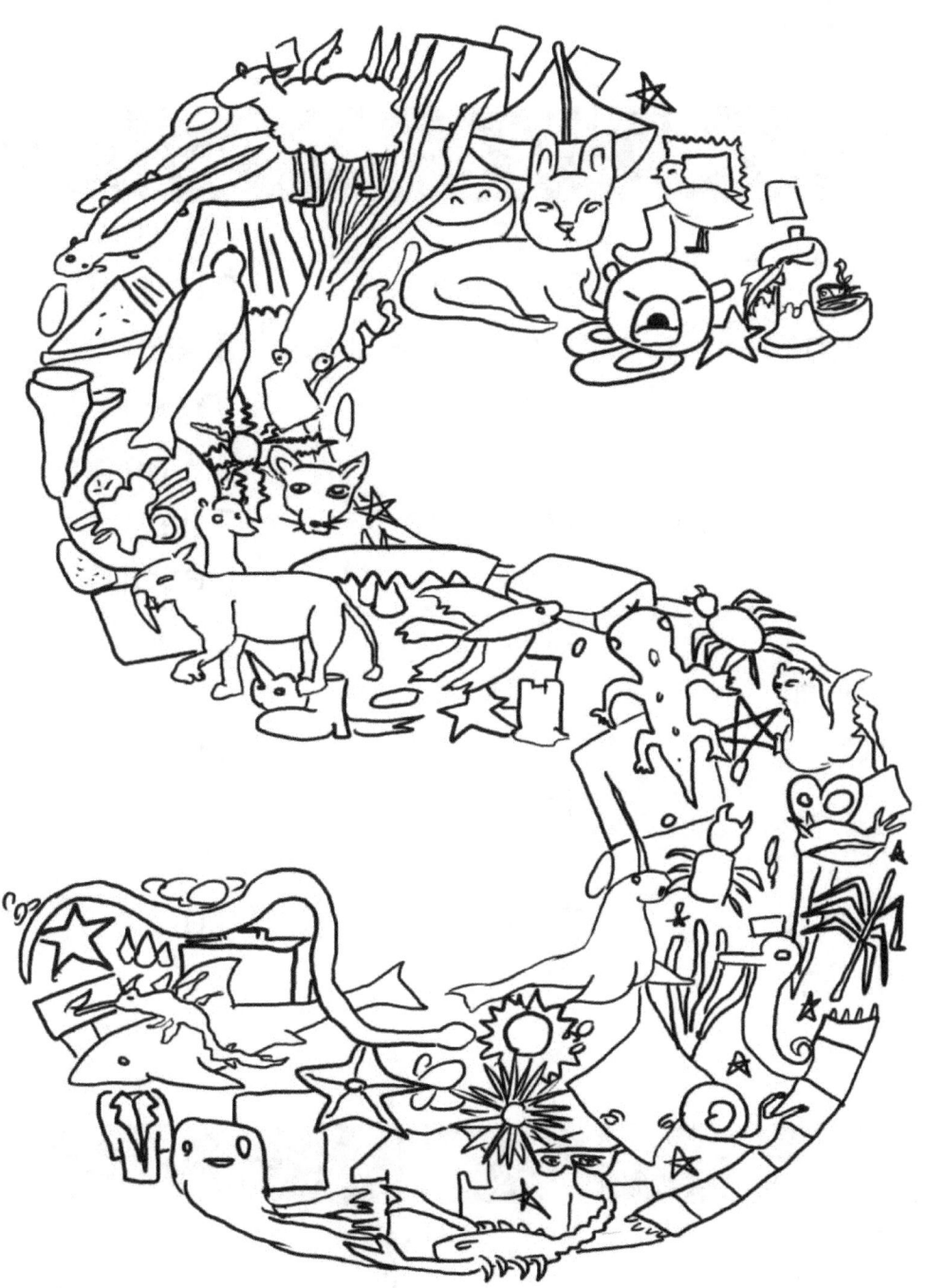

T is for:

Easy to Spot			
Table	Tent	Tortoise	
Taco	Termite	Toucan	
Tamborine	Thorny Devil	Tree	
Tape	Tie	Tree Frog	
Tapir	Tiger	T-Shirt	
Tasmanian Devil	Tiger Shark	Tuatara (reptile)	
Tawny Frogmouth	Toast	Tube	
Teacup	Toe	Tulip	
Teapot	Tomato	Tuna	
Teddy Bear	Tooth	Turkey	
Telephone	Toothbrush	Turtle	
Tennis Ball	Top Hat	TV	

Eagle Eyed		
Tarsier	Tray	
Tart	Tub	

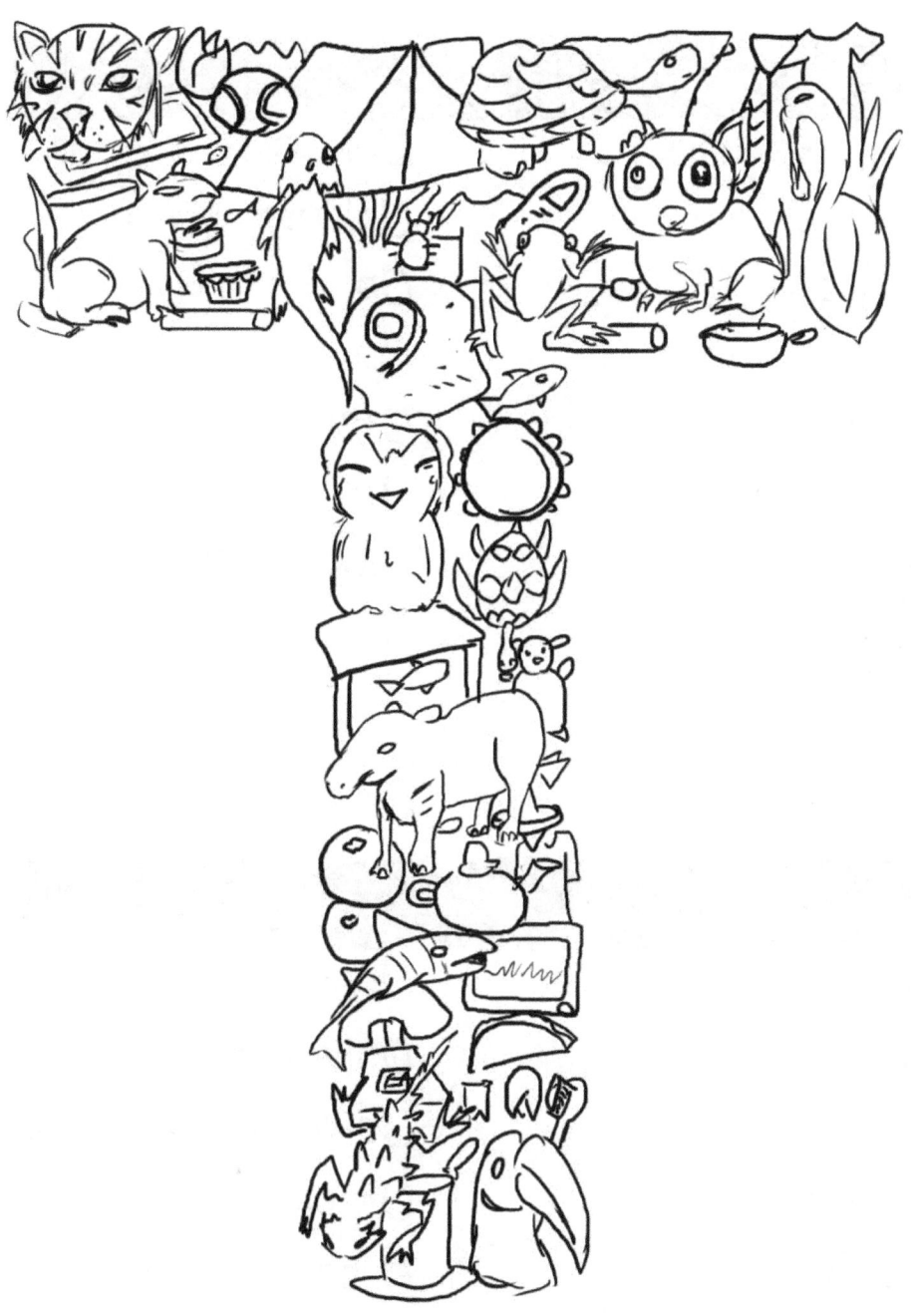

U is for:

Easy to Spot		
Uakari (monkey)	Unicycle	
UFO	Uniform	
UK (flag)	Up	
Ukulele	Upset	
Umbrella	Urchin	
Umbrella Bird	Urn	
Umpire	USA (flag)	
Underwear	Utensil	
Unicorn		

Eagle Eyed		
Upside down	Universe	
Ugly	University	
Ulna	University Graduate	
Ultrasound	Uranus	
Undead	Urban	
Ungulate	Urinal	

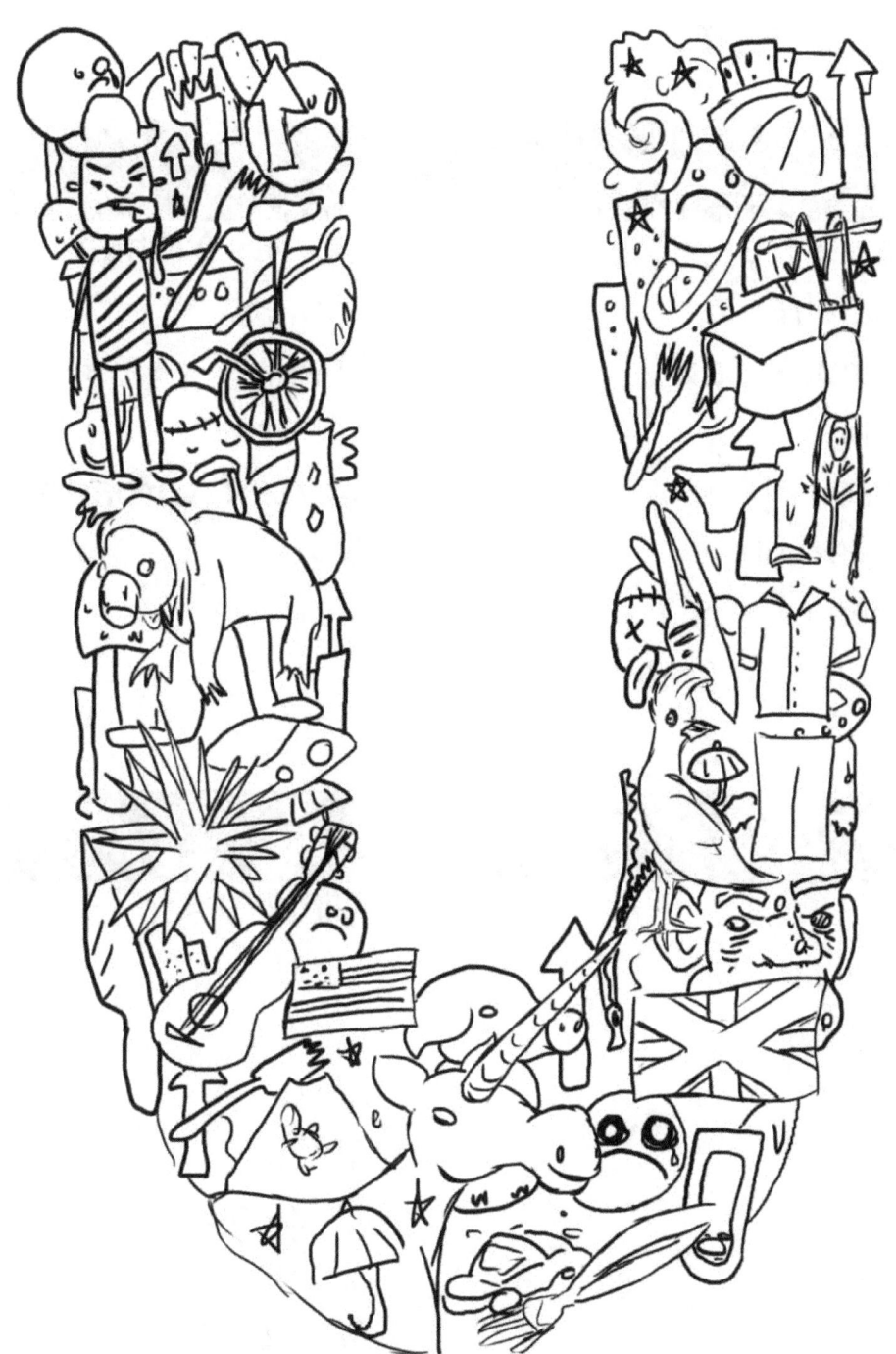

V is for:

Easy to Spot		
Valentine	Vervet Monkey	
Vampire	Violets	
Vampire Bat	Violin	
Van	Viper	
Vase	Vortex (tornado)	
Vegetable	Vote	
Velvet Cupcake	Vulture	
Venus Fly Trap		

Eagle Eyed		
Vacuum	Video Tape	
Vanilla	Vine	
Vegetation	Vinegar	
Velcro	Visor	
Velvet	Voice	
Venus	Volcano	
Vesper	Volleyball	
Vest	Vortex (toy)	

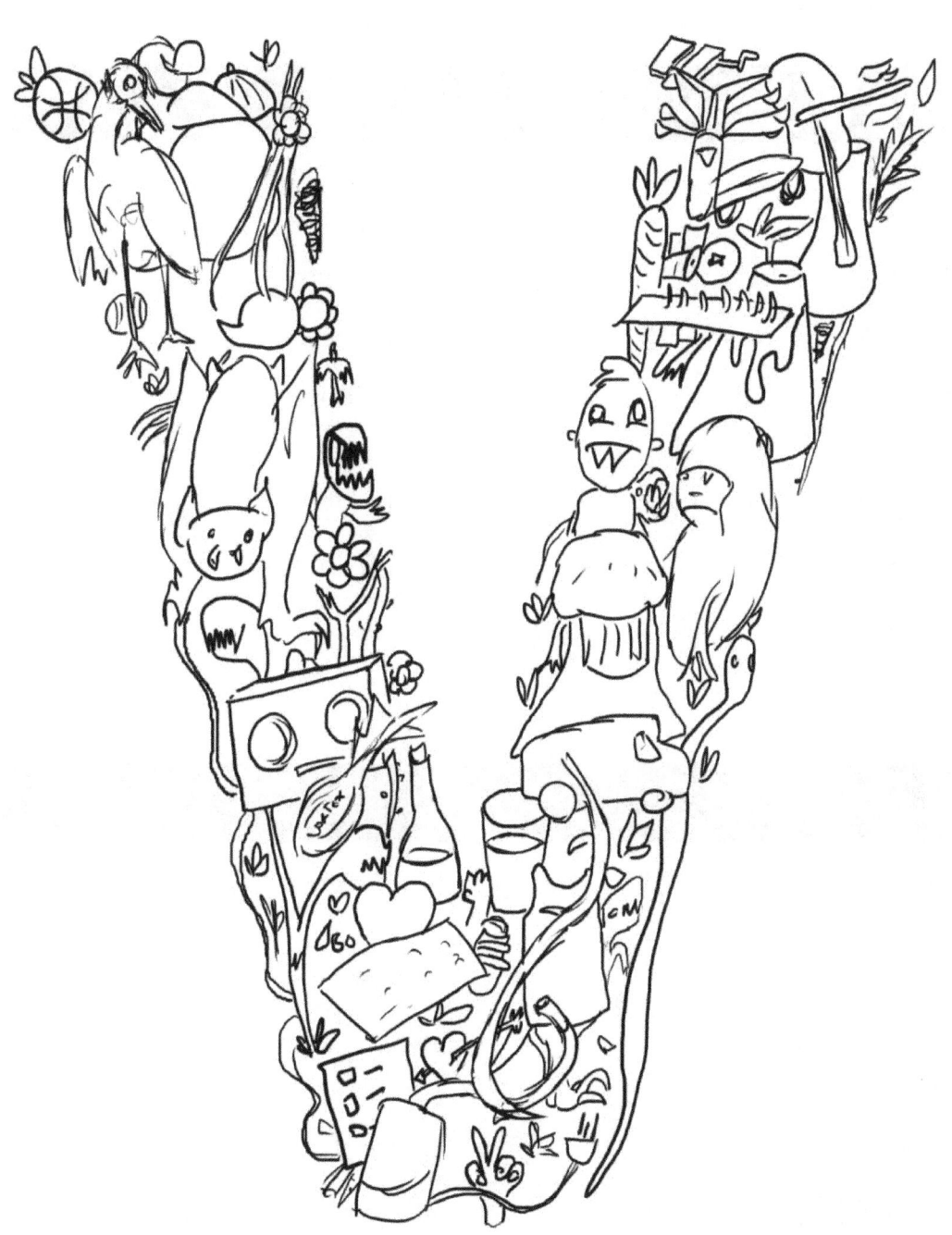

W is for:

Easy to Spot		
Waffle	Wedge	
Wagon	Whale	
Wall	Whippet	
Wallaby	Wildebeest	
Walrus	Windmill	
Wand	Window	
Warthog	Wolf	
Wasp	Wombat	
Watch		

Eagle Eyed		
Wafer	Whip	
Walnut	Wig	
Water	Winter	
Watercolour	Wire	
Watermelon	Witch	
Wave	Wizard	
Wedding Ring	Wok	
West	Wolverine	
Whale Shark	Woolly Mammoth	

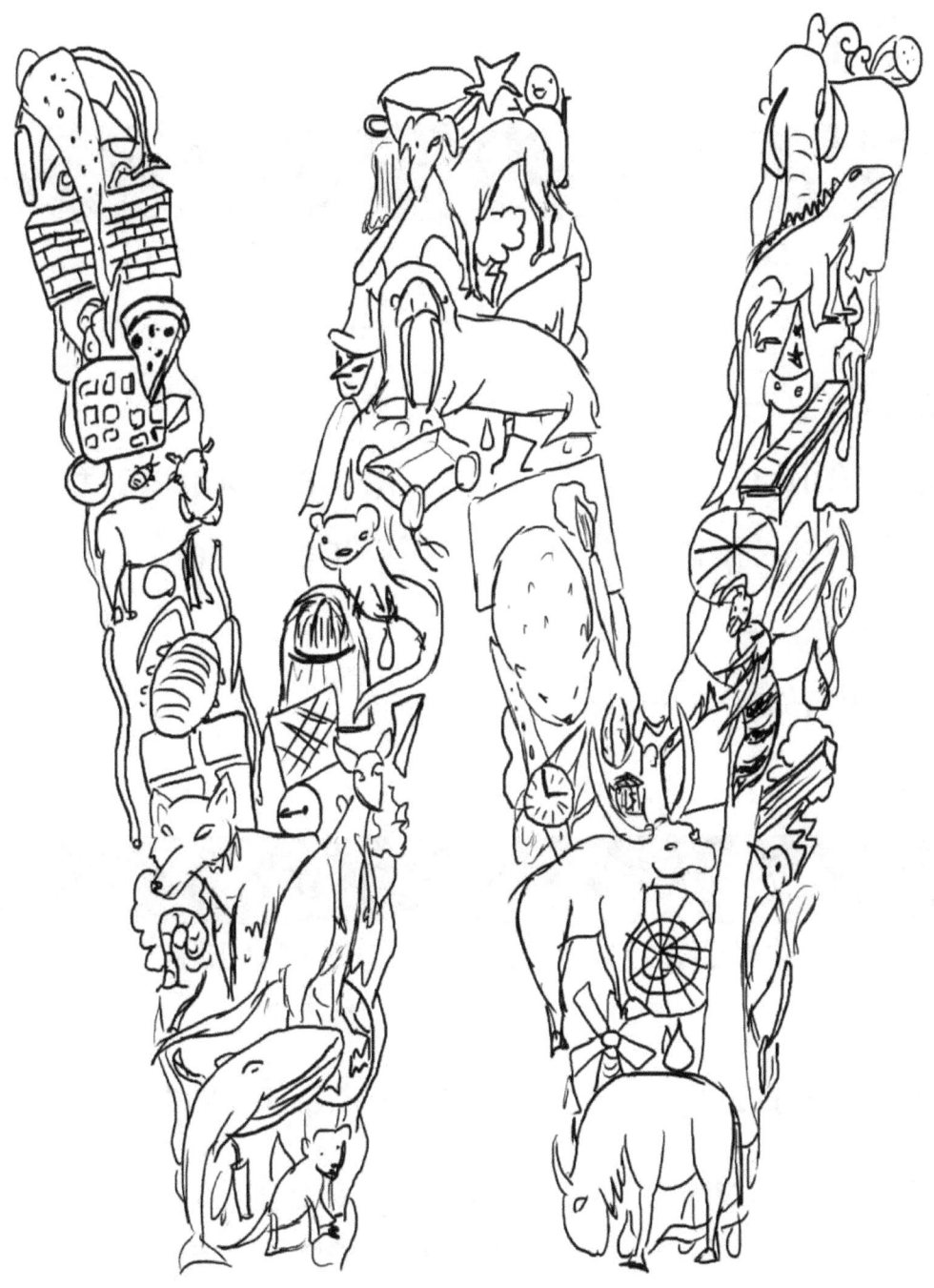

X is for:

Easy to Spot			
Xanadu (plant)		Xoanon (idol)	
Xbox		X-ray	
Xebec (boat)		X-ray Fish	
Xeme (bird)		Xylem (cell part)	
Xerophyte (plant family)		Xylophone	
Xiphias (swordfish)			

Eagle Eyed			
Xenolith (rock)		Xylography (word engraving art)	
Xenon tube		Xylorimba (instrument)	
Xenops (bird)		Xyster (surgical instrument)	
Xerox Machine		Xyston (Greek weapon)	

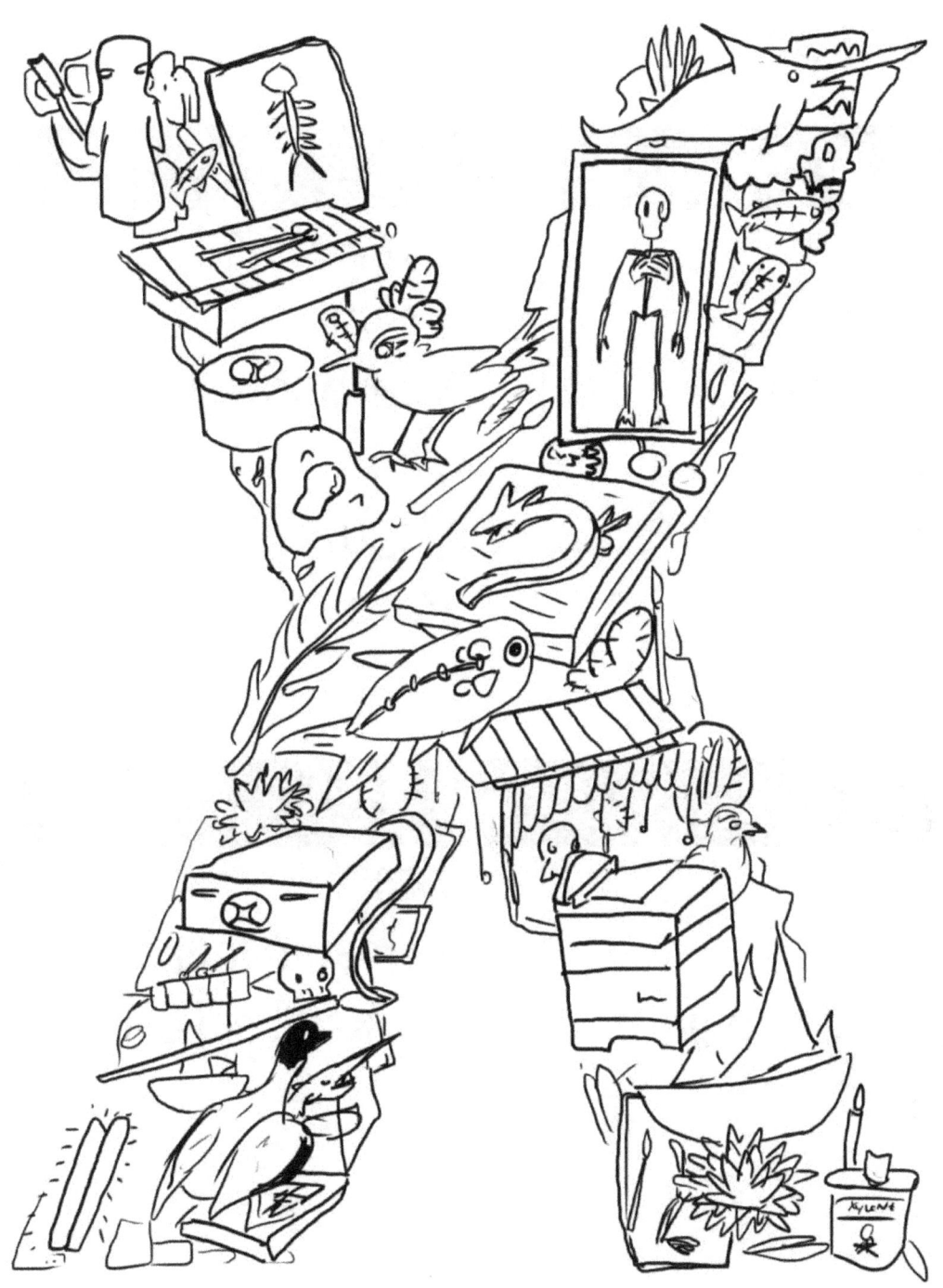

Y is for:

Easy to Spot		
Yacht	Yardstick	
Youth	Yawn	
Yoga Mat	Yearbook	
Yoga	Yen	
Yabby	Yogurt	
Yak	Yoyo	

Eagle Eyed		
Yam	Yeast	
Yarn	Yemen (flag)	
Yarrow (flower)	Yorkshire Terrier	
Year		

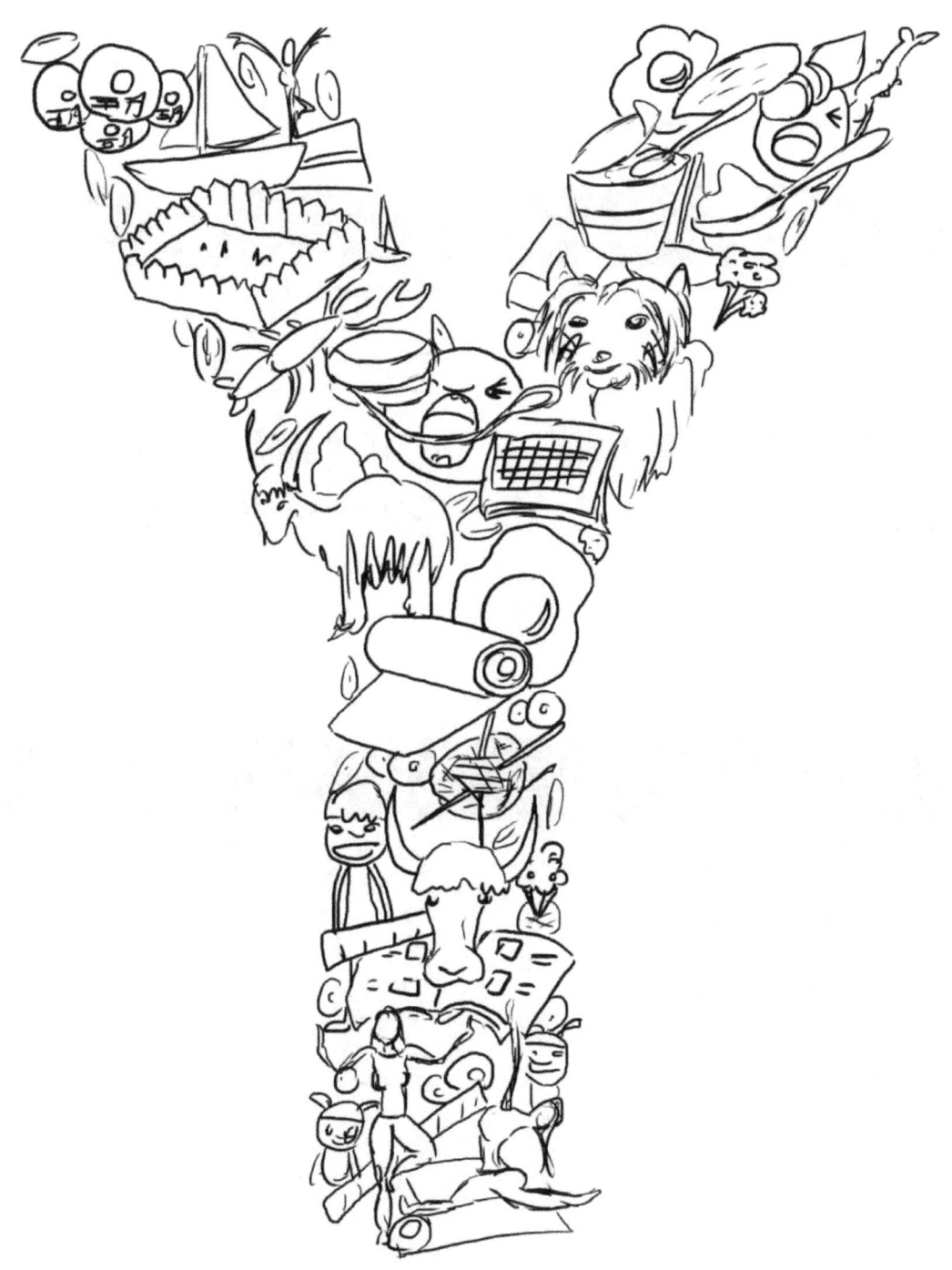

Z is for:

Easy to Spot			
Zebra		Zombie	
Zebra Shark		Zoom Lens	
Zeppelin (blimp)		Zip-Lock Bag	
Zero		Zinnia (flower)	
Zigzag			

Eagle Eyed			
Zither		Zooplankton	
Zodiac Sign		Zorilla	
Zimbabwe (Flag)		Zygote	
Zoo		Zip	

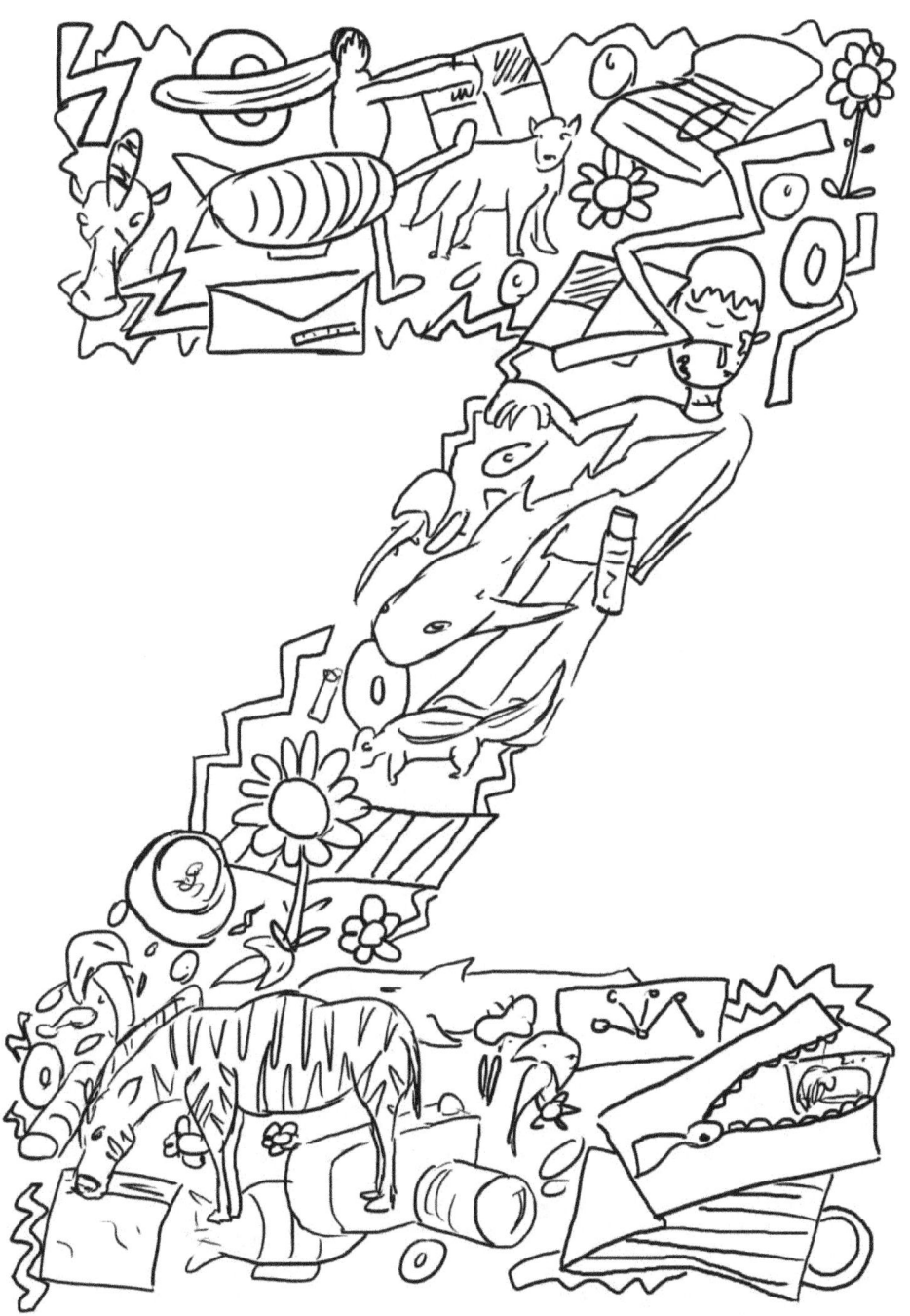

www.ingramcontent.com/pod-product-compliance
Lightning Source LLC
Chambersburg PA
CBHW080608180526
45168CB00007B/2830